IN RECITAL
Throughout the Year™
(with Performance Strategies)
Volume Two

ABOUT THE SERIES • A NOTE TO THE TEACHER

In Recital — Throughout the Year™ is a series that focuses on fabulous repertoire, intended to motivate your students. We know that to motivate, the teacher must challenge the student with attainable goals. This series makes that possible. The fine composers and arrangers of this series have created musically engaging pieces, which have been carefully leveled and address the technical strengths and weaknesses of students. The wide range of styles in each book of the series complements other FJH publications and will help you to plan students' recital repertoire for the entire year. You will find original solos and duets that focus on different musical and technical issues, giving you the selection needed to accommodate your students' needs. There are arrangements of famous classical themes, as well as repertoire written for Halloween, Christmas, and Fourth of July recitals. In this way, your student will have recital pieces throughout the entire year! Additionally, the series provides a progressive discussion on the art of performance. The earlier levels offer tips on recital preparation, while the later levels address more advanced technical and psychological issues that help to realize successful performances.

Use the enclosed CD as a teaching and motivational tool. Have your students listen to the recording and discuss interpretation with you!

Production: Frank and Gail Hackinson
Production Coordinators: Philip Groeber and Isabel Otero Bowen
Cover: Terpstra Design, San Francisco
Cover Piano Illustration: Keith Criss
Engraving: Kevin Olson and Tempo Music Press, Inc.
Printer: Tempo Music Press, Inc.

ISBN 1-56939-479-2

9 RECITAL PREPARATION TIPS • FOR THE TEACHER

1. Consider a tiered approach to developing comfort in performance. Make "mini" performances a regular occurrence, probably without even calling them performances. Have a student play for the student who follows his/her lesson. It doesn't matter if their leveling is different; the older students are naturally nice to the young and the young provide a non-threatening audience for the older. Have students play mini concerts at home. Younger students may enjoy concerts for their favorite stuffed animals each day after practice. Advise older students to practice performing by recording themselves. Of course, you will tailor these suggestions according to each student's personality. Just remember, *no venue is too small and frequency is the key.* Suggestions for mini-performances and performance strategies are also addressed on pages 24, 25, and 42.

   Once students are comfortable with these "mini" performances, teachers must create opportunities for students to play in public, so that they will get used to the idea of getting up on stage and playing for others. Studio group lessons or performance classes are perfect for trial performances, then take it to the next step and invite family or friends to a performance class.

   Try these different performance venues and you will be pleased with the results. The "tiered" approach helps performance to become a natural part of piano study.

2. Make sure that your students have the opportunity to perform pieces well within their technical range. These performances will help build student confidence and will make a huge difference when they are playing more challenging repertoire.

3. Have students practice concentrating on the tempo, mood, and dynamics of the piece before beginning to play.

4. Coach students on how to walk purposefully *to* the piano, adjust the bench, and check their position relative to the piano. Have them practice this a lot in the lesson and at home. Familiarity with the process really helps.

5. Talk to your students about how to finish the piece. Coach them to stay with the music until the piece is over. Discuss how they will move at the end of the piece: i.e., quickly moving the hands away from the keyboard, or slowly lifting the hands with the lifting of the pedal, depending on the repertoire.

6. Coach students how to bow and walk purposefully *away* from the piano. Again, practice this together often so that it feels natural to them.

7. Remind students to keep the recital in perspective. The recital piece should be one of several the student is working on, so that they understand that there is "life after the recital."

8. If possible, have a practice session in the performance location. Encourage your students to focus on what they can control and remind them that although a piano may feel differently, their technique will not "go away."

9. Have your students listen to the companion CD. Not only does this give them ideas on how to interpret the pieces, it builds an intuitive knowledge of how the pieces sound, which helps increase confidence and comfort.

The goal is to instill in our students the excitement of playing for others and to demystify the process. There is nothing quite like communicating a piece of music to an audience and then enjoying their positive reaction to it. With our help, our students can perform up to their potential in public and enjoy this exciting and rewarding experience.

ORGANIZATION OF THE SERIES
IN RECITAL • THROUGHOUT THE YEAR™

*I*n Recital — *Throughout the Year*™ is carefully leveled into the following six categories: Early Elementary, Elementary, Late Elementary, Early Intermediate, Intermediate, and Late Intermediate. Each of the works has been selected for its artistic as well as its pedagogical merit.

Book Six — Late Intermediate, reinforces the following concepts:

- Rhythmic patterns of dotted eighth notes, triplets, and sixteenth notes.

- Pieces in simple, compound, and mixed meters.

- More challenging passage work, scales in tenths, octaves, glissandos, and hand over hand configurations.

- An introduction to the rhythms and style of Spanish music.

- Pieces with changes of tempo, character, and articulations.

- Students play pieces in which the melody and the accompaniment are found within the same hand.

- Syncopated rhythms, jazz chords, and all kinds of arpeggiated and broken chord patterns.

- Simple ornamentation is used such as grace notes and trills.

- Pieces reinforce the following musical terms: *espressivo, semplice, secco, più animato, appassionato, più mosso, meno mosso, con passione controllata, accelerando, rallentando*, along with basic musical terminology found in books 1-5.

- A mixture of major and minor keys strengthen a student's command of the piano.

In addition to the solo pieces in this book, there are two equal part duets: *Rags to Riches*, and *El Velorio*.

TABLE OF CONTENTS

for Sergio Monsevais
Tango Romántico

Timothy Brown

FF1557

10

RAGS TO RICHES
Secondo

Kevin Olson

RAGS TO RICHES
Primo

Kevin Olson

Full of energy (♩ = 152-160)

FF1557

Secondo

Primo

Secondo

Primo

A Stormy Voyage

Christopher Goldston

18

Jazz Etude

Kevin Olson

Quick and driving, with even eighth notes (♩ = 132-144)

MANAGING PERFORMANCE JITTERS

Here are a few things to think about before you perform. It is important to think about them well in advance of the performance, so that you feel great about the performance when it comes!

The greatest freedom in playing comes from the most disciplined preparation...

- **Stay** in the moment.

- **Don't** judge yourself.

- **Don't** think of what happened or what might happen.

- **Think** about the importance of a steady beat and an appropriate tempo.

- **Concentrate** on what you can control, and don't worry about what you can't.

- **Assess** your performance after you play, not *during*.

- **Think** positive scenarios about your playing; then imagine yourself playing your recital piece beautifully.

- **Keep** the performance in perspective and enjoy it! Every performance is a learning experience!

You can use these pages as a practice guide for every recital piece you play in this book!

Preparing for a recital is like throwing darts at the bull's eye.

Follow these practice steps:

- Mark off small sections of your recital piece. Play one of the sections. Every time you play something incorrectly, mark a place on one of the circles of the dartboard around the bull's eye. If you play something absolutely correctly, mark the bull's eye. When you miss the bull's eye we call it "learning" the piece. When you can hit the bull's eye consistently, then you are "practicing."

- Try to earn a "bull's eye" five times in a row, practicing the exact same small section of your recital piece.

- The more you practice, the better your mark will be at earning a bull's eye. Soon you will be able to get a bull's eye 6 times in a row, or 7, or 8 times! Use this strategy, it works!

To learn **What Makes a Performance Stellar**, turn to page 42.

FF1557

to Jón Sigurdsson and Family

SUNRISE OVER REYKJAVIK

This piece was inspired by an early morning walk by the North Sea in Reykjavik, Iceland.
The sky was lit with pinks and oranges, stretching out over the water.
There was one bird, soaring high above the quiet city.

Wynn-Anne Rossi

Reflective (♩ = ca. 66)

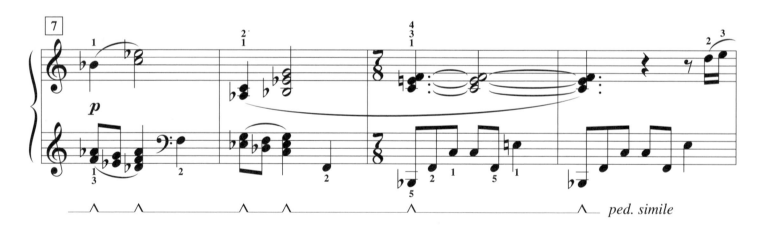

ped. simile

It Came Upon the Midnight Clear

Richard Storrs Willis
arr. Melody Bober

Calmly, freely (♩ = ca. 92)

31

FF1557

El Velorio

Secondo

Ignacio Cervantes
arr. Edwin McLean

Moderato (♪ = 144-160)

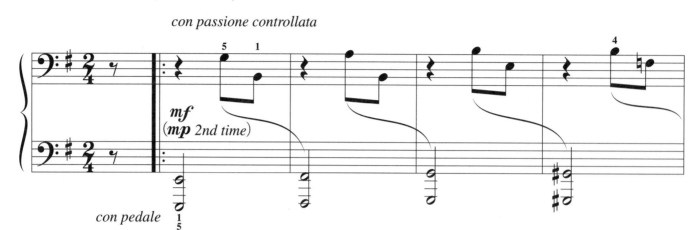

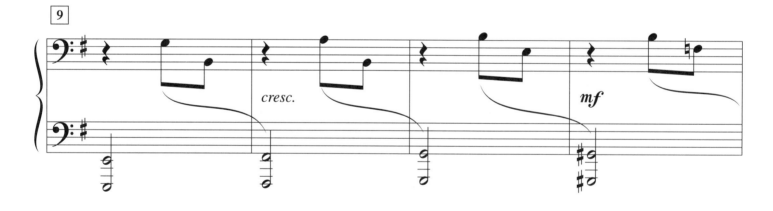

FF1557

El Velorio
Primo

Ignacio Cervantes
arr. Edwin McLean

FF1557

Secondo

Primo

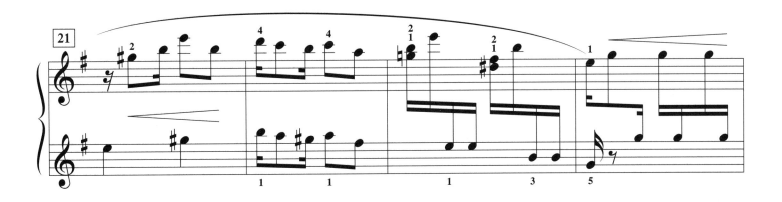

JESU, JOY OF MAN'S DESIRING

Johann Sebastian Bach
arr. Kevin Costley

Flowing, lyrically, not rushed (♩ = 69-76)

40

FF1557

WHAT MAKES A PERFORMANCE STELLAR?

Starting four weeks before your actual performance, practice the following performance strategies every day. It might be difficult to do all of these at first, but the more you practice, the easier they will become. Remember, if you prepare well, the performance day will be easy and your playing will amaze your audience!

Place a check in the box each day you complete the task.

4 weeks	3 weeks	2 weeks	1 week

Can you play the entire piece, hands alone? (Listening to each individual part helps you to be completely aware of what each hand is playing.)

Can you sing or hum the melody away from the piano?

Can you start your piece at four *different* places in the music? (You and your teacher can mark with a star ☆ four good starting places).

Can you play the piece from beginning to end at "half tempo"? ("Half tempo" means to play it with all of the correct rhythms, notes, and dynamics, but at half of the speed you would play it when performing it.)

After playing the piece, ask yourself: Did it sound like the title suggests? Did I bring the piece to life?

Other questions you can ask yourself:

- Do I play all of the dynamics as the composer intended them to be?
- Do I play with all of the correct articulations? (not too sticky or too quick)
- Do I give the notes their exact duration?
- Are the *ritardandos* and *accelerandos* in the right places?
- Is my sound beautiful?
- Is my passage work clear?
- Have I worked to control all of the soft or slow passages?
- Can I play my recital piece without the pedal — dry and with complete accuracy?

You can use this page as a practice guide for every recital piece you play in this book!

ABOUT THE COMPOSERS/ARRANGERS

Melody Bober

Piano instructor, music teacher, composer, clinician—Melody Bober has been active in music education for over 25 years. As a composer, her goal is to create exciting and challenging pieces that are strong teaching tools to promote a lifelong love, understanding, and appreciation for music. Pedagogy, ear training, and musical expression are fundamentals of Melody's teaching, as well as fostering composition skills in her students.

Melody graduated with highest honors from the University of Illinois with a degree in music education, and later received a master's degree in piano performance. She maintains a large private studio, performs in numerous regional events, and conducts workshops across the country. She and her husband Jeff reside in Minnesota.

Timothy Brown

Composition has always been a natural form of self-expression for Timothy Brown. His Montessori-influenced philosophy has greatly helped define his approach as a teacher and composer of educational music. His composition originates from a love of improvisation at the piano and his personal goal of writing music that will help release the student's imagination.

Mr. Brown holds two degrees in piano performance, including a master's degree from the University of North Texas. His many honors include a "Commissioned for Clavier" magazine article, and first prize award in the Fifth Aliénor International Harpsichord Competition for his solo composition *Suite Española*. As a clinician, Mr. Brown has presented numerous clinics and most recently represented FJH Music with his presentation at the 2000 World Piano Pedagogy Conference. Currently living in Dallas, Mr. Brown teaches piano and composition at the Harry Stone Montessori Magnet School. He frequently serves as an adjudicator for piano and composition contests, and performs with his wife as duo-pianists.

Kevin Costley

Kevin Costley holds several graduate degrees in the areas of elementary education and piano pedagogy, and literature, including a doctorate from Kansas State University. For nearly two decades, he was owner and director of The Keyboard Academy, specializing in innovative small group instruction. Kevin served for several years as head of the music department and on the keyboard faculty of Messenger College in Joplin, Missouri.

Kevin is a standing faculty member of Inspiration Point Fine Arts Colony piano and string camp, where he performs and teaches private piano, ensemble classes, and composition. He conducts child development seminars, writes for national publications, serves as a clinician for piano workshops, and adjudicates numerous piano festivals and competitions.

Christopher Goldston

Christopher Goldston holds a Master of Music degree in piano performance and pedagogy from Northwestern University, and a Bachelor of Music degree in piano performance from the University of North Carolina–Greensboro. He lives in Chicago, Illinois, and has taught at Sherwood Conservatory of Music and Harper College.

In 1991, Mr. Goldston received the National Federation of Music Clubs Lynn Freeman Olson Composition Award for his first composition, *Night Train*. Since then, he has written numerous pieces for piano, voice, and chamber ensemble, including *Thesis for Wind Quintet,* which won the 1993 North Carolina State Music Teachers Association Collegiate Composition Contest.

Mr. Goldston has taught piano for over ten years and enjoys composing and arranging pieces for his students. Many of them have created pieces of their own under his guidance and have received top prizes in state competitions. Mr. Goldston has also served as chair of the composition contest for Illinois State Music Teachers Association and MTNA East Central Division.

Edwin McLean

Edwin McLean is a freelance composer living in Chapel Hill, North Carolina. He is a graduate of the Yale School of Music, where he studied with Krzysztof Penderecki and Jacob Druckman. He also holds a master's degrees in music theory and a bachelor's degree in piano performance from the University of Colorado.

The recipient of several grants and awards: The MacDowell Colony, the John Work Award, the Woods Chandler Prize (Yale), Meet the Composer, Florida Arts Council, and others, he has also won the Aliénor Composition Competition for his work *Sonata for Harpsichord*, published by The FJH Music Company and recorded by Elaine Funaro (*Into the Millennium*, Gasparo GSCD-331).

Since 1979, Edwin McLean has arranged the music of some of today's best known recording artists. Currently, he is senior editor as well as MIDI orchestrator for FJH Music.

Kevin Olson

Kevin Olson is an active pianist, composer, and faculty member at Elmhurst College near Chicago, Illinois, where he teaches classical and jazz piano, music theory, and electronic music. He holds a Doctor of Education degree from National-Louis University, and bachelor's and master's degrees in music composition and theory from Brigham Young University. Before teaching at Elmhurst College, he held a visiting professor position at Humboldt State University in California.

A native of Utah, Kevin began composing at the age of five. When he was twelve, his composition *An American Trainride* received the Overall First Prize at the 1983 National PTA Convention in Albuquerque, New Mexico. Since then, he has been a composer-in-residence at the National Conference on Piano Pedagogy and has written music for the American Piano Quartet, Chicago a cappella, the Rich Matteson Jazz Festival, among others. Kevin maintains a large piano studio, teaching students of a variety of ages and abilities. Many of the needs of his own piano students have inspired over forty books and solos published by The FJH Music Company Inc., which he joined as a writer in 1994.

Wynn-Anne Rossi

Wynn-Anne Rossi is a multitalented composer, pianist, and educator. According to the Illinois Times, which awarded her the accolade Best Piano Teacher, she is "about as conventional as her hyphenated first name."

A resident of Minnesota, Wynn-Anne has received commissions from Minnesota Public Radio, America Composers Forum, Minnesota Music Teachers Association, and a number of private institutions. She is currently being presented as a living woman composer by the Bravo Music Education Program, which introduces her original works to thousands of elementary children each year. She also enjoys presenting lectures on various topics, including the art of incorporating original composition into piano study.

Educated at the University of Colorado in theory and composition, Wynn-Anne has traveled and lived throughout the United States. In Boston, she furthered her training at Harvard University. She has written a wide variety of repertoire, including a futuristic ballet, children's liturgical music, text and music for vocal ensembles, and chamber music.